Winning the Exhibition Game II
Keep on Winning!

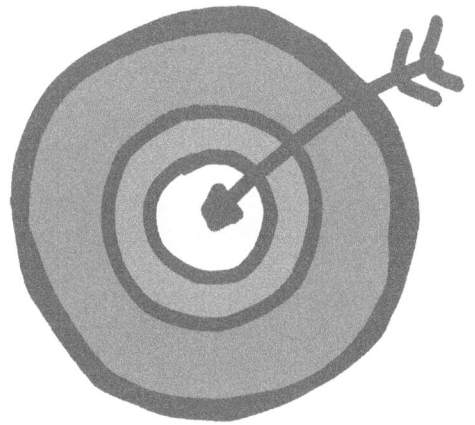

On Target Books

Winning the Exhibition Game II
Keep on Winning!

by
Jim Ewan

Published by
On Target Books, Ty Isaf,
Newchapel, Boncath SA37 0EH.
Wales

First published 2003. Revised edition published
2013. All rights reserved. No part of this work
may be reproduced or stored in an information
retrieval system (other than for purposes of
review) without the express permission of the
publisher in writing.

This book is *still* for Katie Cakeshop –
my inspiration and my proofreader.
(So any typos are her fault!)

Contents

Preface to the 2nd edition

Ten years - and a lot of water under the bridge.

So what has changed? Well, the industry has contracted alarmingly – by as much as 25% according to some sources. The reason is simple to understand – exhibitors are not seeing a worthwhile return on investment. In times of plenty they manage to ignore this or rationalise their continued attendance; as the economic situation worsens though, anyone with any sense begins to question the waste of money.

So far as those still exhibiting are concerned, sadly there seems very little improvement. I still see them making the same mistakes I made forty years ago. And I continue my crusade to bring sanity and success to those willing to listen!

There is encouragement to be had from *organisers* however. I was very cruel (justifiably) to them in the original book. Now I see many actually taking an interest in their clients' results. In extreme cases, some organisers are even mounting workshops and arranging helpline-type support. Maybe things are looking up after all.

Preface to the 1st edition

Early in the century before last, a dedicated and hard-working missionary was on an extended tour of Africa. One day he was preaching at a remote village and he was *mustard!* The villagers were full of enthusiasm and greeted every rousing proclamation with raised arms and an admiring cry of "Umbongo!" Each time they did so the missionary was spurred on to greater heights of passion and religious fervour.

Eventually, soaked in sweat, and exhausted yet elated, he bade farewell to the headman and prepared to continue on to the next village. At the edge of the village the headman pointed the way, which happened to take the missionary though a field full of cattle.

The missionary waved and turned to go. "By the way," warned the headman, "mind you don't step in the umbongo."

There is a lot of umbongo associated with the business of exhibiting. Much of it generated by exhibition organisers, those supremely confident beings who will assure you that the best possible place to sell steel ball bearings is at the Ideal Home Show.

Who insist that being absent from the World Plumbing Symposium will mean the instant demise of your wholesale flower business. Exhibitors themselves also spread umbongo, whether it be by exaggerating the success of their stand or bemoaning the inadequacies of the aforementioned organisers. This book aims to expose the waffle and emphasise the essentials. Here you will find templates, formulae and tips that will ease your mind, your pocket and your progress towards the perfect exhibition.

I know – it's exciting, isn't it? Compose yourself and read on.

Introduction

Exhibiting at trade shows is hard work – and fun. It is expensive – and effective. Or at least it should be. So how come something like 30% of first-time exhibitors vow never to repeat the experience?

I suggest it is because they have not properly thought out what they wanted nor planned how they were going to get it. They simply booked a space, built a stand and waited for the miracle to happen. The miracle workers being, of course, the exhibition organisers. They were supposed to ensure that a flood tide of prospects appeared demanding the services or products on display and flourishing their plastic like dowagers at a Harrods sale. Sadly, it doesn't work that way. The job of the organiser is to bring in the crowds, yes. But it is *your* job, as exhibitor, to attract people, the right people, to your particular stand.

How to achieve that nirvana? That is what this book will show you. Winning the exhibition game is simple. Not easy, of course, but simple. Follow the rules, learn from the mistakes of others and soon you will be smiling all the way to wherever it is you would like to smile all the way to. Barbados does it for me.

Jim Ewan

January 2003 (Now it's 2012 and I have nothing to add!)

P.S. Very often when I read a book I find myself irritated by the author's foibles. In order to reduce the irritation factor of this book, you may like to know the following:

I refer to people who use services or buy products as 'clients'. This is, of course, a conceit and you may prefer 'customer',' buyer', 'mug' or whatever. But I like to think that 'client' is a friendlier label and reflects a closer, longer-lasting relationship than do the other terms.

I use the pronouns 'him', 'her', 'his', 'hers' etc. at random. This means nothing and the terms are generally interchangeable. If you are sad enough to count, you will probably find I use masculine terms more frequently than feminine ones. That's because I'm male and I was brought up in sexist times. I'm doing my best to be a new man but it ain't easy learning new tricks when you're an old dog. Have patience.

Finally, you may find I don't treat business as seriously as some people think I should. That's because business is a game (like life) and in my opinion games shouldn't be taken seriously. You are entitled to disagree but you can't have your money back. That's life!

Chapter 1

Why should *you* exhibit?

I remember the first trade show I ever attended as an exhibitor. It was a big London computer show in the early 1970s. And it was like a bad dream. I was the Marketing Director of a successful computer consultancy and yet I had no real idea of why we were exhibiting – it just seemed the thing to do. Our company had grown swiftly during the boom times of the sixties; we had gone international; we *deserved* to be seen at the industry's premier event.

Our stand was pretty basic; some pictures of the directors talking to important clients, a couple of chairs and a table on which copies of our company brochure were tastefully arranged (so tastefully that no visitor dared disturb their symmetry by taking one).

The company name was blazoned across the back of the stand in six-inch thick foam. Late the night before opening someone realised that nowhere on the stand did we reveal anything about our services. A graphics man had to be called in to solve the problem. Three hours at a considerable hourly premium seemed a small price to pay to cover our gaffe.

Winning the Exhibition Game II
Keep on Winning!

As it was the seventies we naturally had pretty girls in short skirts handing out literature by the lorry load. We got tons of coverage in the computer press, all of it concerning the pretty girls. We also got no business whatsoever. At least no business so far as we knew, because, of course, we had no system arranged to evaluate the results of our efforts.

Our entire sales force, seven strong, wasted a week (only the exhibition week since few of the 'leads' we garnered were ever followed up) and we vowed never to repeat the disastrous experiment.

Yes, friend, I have made all the mistakes! If you listen to my clients, it seems I have learned from them – luckily or this book would not be much help to you.

So – why should *you* exhibit?

There are some very good reasons. Before we discuss them though, I'd like to talk about the *wrong* reasons for exhibiting. Why? Because you would be amazed at the number of times they are the only reasons offered. So here they are (I have avoided the temptation to dismiss each 'reason' with a simple cry of "Umbongo!")

Winning the Exhibition Game II
Keep on Winning!

The competition will be exhibiting. (This is also sometimes offered as a reason for not going.)

Either way, it's irrelevant.

We want the exposure.

There are cheaper ways to get exposure.

We're running one of the seminar sessions.

Do you really need a stand as well? This could be a perfect way to get 'exposure' without the cost of exhibiting.

We've always been there.

Oh, dear.

People will notice if we don't have a stand.

No they won't.

We're going in order to show support for our trade organisation.

Write them a cheque; it'll be cheaper in the long run.

Winning the Exhibition Game II
Keep on Winning!

We'll meet all our colleagues from around the country (world).

This seems to be the main objective of many stand staff – to renew acquaintances and party the nights away. No wonder they don't attract visitors to the stand, they're too busy with each other or their hangovers to give visitors a second glance.

Because the show is in Ibiza.

Take your holidays on your own time.

It helps maintain our image.

Oh, yeah?

It offers an opportunity to train new sales staff.

You should train them <u>first</u>, you klutz!

Any of these reasons will almost certainly mean that the show will be at best a loss leader for you. Is this acceptable? Only you and your financial director can answer that. From my experience of financial directors, my bet is that the answer is 'NO!' in seven-foot high neon letters.

Winning the Exhibition Game II
Keep on Winning!

In truth, though I have seen lists several dozen items long, there are but three main reasons to exhibit:

> To make new sales
> To make appointments
> To make new contacts

There are also some subsidiary reasons:

> To raise awareness of your product/service
> To do some market research
> To do some industry research
> To introduce new products/services to the market
> To recruit staff/agents/distributors

But none of these subsidiary reasons alone is likely to justify the cost.

So what exactly makes exhibitions so worthwhile?

Let's look at the exhibition visitors. 30% of them will be directors or senior managers – with purchasing authority. 35% of them will be relatively new to their job – and so may be looking to forge new supplier relationships. Think about that. You will meet prospective clients who are probably a couple of ranks above those your sales staff are currently chasing and, moreover, a third of them are probably looking for alternative suppliers. Nowhere else will you find that kind of quality prospect gathered in such numbers. You are like a shopaholic with a platinum card let loose in Knightsbridge. Consider:

According to surveys*, 63% of sales and marketing managers say shows help to gain market share. Odd since 80% of leads are still not followed up! And yet 77% of qualified attendees are potential customers.
*UFI; USAToday; Leelentz

Curiously, CEIR says that 77% is also the percentage of marketeers value business-to-business shows for their ability to generate new sales leads!

The Association of Exhibition Organisers found, in 2002, that 29% of visitors *only* see sales representatives at exhibitions. So trade exhibitions will reveal to you those buyers you never knew existed. And they are unencumbered by gatekeepers, switchboard operators or PAs trying to shield them from your approach.

> *Your sales people no doubt spend countless hours researching, writing and phoning to try to discover the*

*right contact at the right organisation
to whom they can make their pitch.
Having found out whom they need to
talk to, they have to face a minefield
of 'rejectionists' intent on stopping
them doing their job. This exercise
can resemble trying to fight your way
out of Hampton Court Maze on a dark
winter's night - cold, mysterious and
prickly. Far better to have them come
to you.*

At an exhibition the *right* people come to
you. Not only that, they come to you eager to
do business and to forge new relationships.
No senior executive goes to a show for fun.
Sure, junior staff may see it as a relaxing day
out of the office; their seniors view it as a
chore that has to be completed and they
want value in return for the time they are
sacrificing. Show them how your service or
your product can help them and they will
reward you handsomely.

Given the above, you need to make sure you
have your best exhibition staff on parade.
This does not mean Fiona from Accounts
because she is a bit slack at present.
(Surprisingly, it probably doesn't mean Brian,
your hottest salesman, either. But more of
that in Chapter 9.)

Winning the Exhibition Game II
Keep on Winning!

According to surveys, the vast majority of exhibition visitors have not been called on by a salesperson during the several months preceding the show. Whether this is because your team has been unsuccessful in locating them or they have been too well protected by the human firewall surrounding all decision makers these days matters not. The fact is they are now available and that is good news for you.

You may say at this point, "Ah, yes, they are at the show, but so are all my competitors. Surely this is a bad thing?" To which I answer, "Only if your service or product is umbongo."

If you were selling food, who would be your ideal customer? Would you believe me if I said "A hungry person"? And where will you find most hungry people with money in their pockets? Perhaps near a restaurant? Which is why restaurants huddle together. And book shops. And shoe shops. And … well, I guess you get the idea. All these competitors would not be in close proximity to one another unless they found it good for business.

Provided you have a good product or service you have no reason to fear the competition. Your clients all shop around anyway, believe me. It's just a little more convenient to do one's comparison-shopping at a show. In fact, close to three-quarters of visitors apparently come to exhibitions to compare offerings. If you aren't there, you can't be part of the comparison.

Other reasons visitors give for attending trade shows include making face-to-face contact with potential suppliers and viewing product demonstrations. And over 60% of exhibition visitors report that they are glad they attended. The other 40% presumably hated every minute and are never going to another exhibition for as long as they live. But three out of five ain't bad. In fact I'd lay odds it's better than your top salesperson's closing rate. (Actually, should your top salesperson's closing rate indeed be better than three out of five, here's a tip for you: *put your prices up.*)

What about the cost of exhibiting? Surprisingly, though exhibitions are costly affairs – and don't let anyone tell you different – they are also cost-effective. According to those surveys again, it takes an average of 3½ calls to close a sale from an exhibition lead but 4½ from other forms of marketing. So what are you waiting for?

Winning the Exhibition Game II
Keep on Winning!

An exhibition is the only form of marketing that brings hot prospects straight to your 'door'. It gives you an unprecedented opportunity to build relationships, demonstrate your products and make your pitch to a whole range of prospects without moving more than a few metres. And it does so at a fraction of the cost of capturing those prospects in the normal day-to-day run of advertising, PR, e-mailing & snail-mailing, telephoning, visiting and generally driving yourself and your team into the ground that is the alternative.

REMEMBER

There are many bad reasons to exhibit

There are three good reasons to exhibit:

> **To make new sales**
> **To make new appointments**
> **To make new contacts**

Senior people (decision makers) go to trade shows

Exhibitions are costly

Exhibitions are (can be) cost-effective

Chapter 2

What do you really want to achieve?

In Chapter One I said there are only three real reasons for exhibiting (plus a few subsidiary ones):

> To make sales
> To make appointments
> To make contacts

At the exhibition you will meet clients and prospects face-to-face. You will meet people not usually accessible to you and your sales team. Importantly, you will be meeting these people on relatively neutral territory, where neither of you need feel disadvantaged.

You will have the opportunity to demonstrate new products, especially products that you cannot conveniently lug around to your prospects' offices, like tanks or sewage filtration systems.

You can make the surroundings much more conducive to developing a long-term relationship than is your dreary old factory. Seduction is the name of the game!

Winning the Exhibition Game II
Keep on Winning!

(Though, speaking of seduction, fear not for your own virtue. While it is true that many real romances begin at exhibitions, these are generally found among the younger staff – not mature old warhorses like you and me. What's that? You're not an old warhorse? Then you will find exhibitions more fun than you ever thought possible.)

So, with all this potential, what are your targets going to be? As I don't know you or your business, I suggest we take a hypothetical company marketing, say, a CRM (customer relationship management) software package that retails at £2500. We'll call the company 'Business Wizardry Ltd' simply because I can't think of a more appropriate name. Their trading style is BizWiz and their aims, at an imaginary 3-day business-to-business exhibition, dreamt up at a board meeting the week before as is traditional, are:

1. Sell £200,000 of product.
2. Make 200 new contacts.
3. Make six appointments for each of their five person sales team.

Is this realistic? Starting with objective number one, let's consider the visitors. The average visitor stays at a show for around four hours. As this includes coffee, lunch and loo breaks, let's call it three hours. There may be 200-300 stands of which 80% will be instantly rejected as being of no interest so she will swiftly pass them over. That leaves around 40-60 stands to visit in three hours – 3-4½ minutes per stand. Is anyone going to spend £2500 on complex software after a 4½-minute presentation? I think not. On to targets 2 and 3 then.

Here we should question the method used to reach these targets. If BizWiz is an average firm, they were plucked out of the air because they "sounded about right". So let us ignore them and instead adopt a more scientific approach.

First we need to know what the outlay ('investment') will be. BizWiz has decided on a 3m X 2m shell stand. Depending on the show, the cost can be anything from less than £200 to more than £400 per square metre. So let us assume £300, or a total of £1800 for their $6m^2$ stand.

A rough rule of thumb says multiply space cost by four to arrive at the total show cost. So BizWiz is looking at an investment of £7200. Add a bit for unexpected contingencies and call it £8000.

Winning the Exhibition Game II
Keep on Winning!

Now to get a return on investment (the famous 'R.O.I.')

BizWiz makes a profit of 50% or £1250 on its product. So to break even we must achieve sales of 6.4 – call it 7 – packages.

BizWiz knows it has a closing ratio of 3:1. Its sales people have to visit three 'warm' prospects to sell one CRM package. So it will take 21 appointments from this show to produce the required break-even income.

The firm also knows it can expect to get a face-to-face meeting with one of every two visitors who leave their stand enthused about the product (2:1). And one in four of the people initially engaged with will become enthused (4:1).

Pulling the above figures together it is easy to see that BizWiz staff must engage with 168 show visitors to make 7 sales (24 engagements = 6 'enthused' = 3 appointments = 1 sale).

These are their figures, of course. You will need to substitute your own statistics – if you know them. But do not despair if, like most organisations, yours does not have the information; the figures quoted above are, perhaps surprisingly, pretty standard across a wide range of businesses.

Next we should consider whether the stand team can actually engage with that number of visitors.

The show is on for two days, from 10am until 5pm – a total of 14 hours. On average then, 12 engagements per hour. If BizWiz has four staff on stand at all times, two can be generating visitors at the rate of one every five minutes, one will be making the mini-presentation required to create enthusiasm and one will be collecting contact information for the follow-up.

So far things are looking good. But it doesn't answer the basic question – "Is it worthwhile exhibiting?" Since this question is invariably asked by the Financial Director, we know he really means, "Will it make us any money?"

What we have concentrated on is break-even figures. How could we improve things to realise a profit?

The first thing to do, obviously, is to factor in the lifetime value of these new customers. BizWiz has an annual support and maintenance contract that adds a further £200 a year and customers tend to remain involved for 3 – 5 years. However, this does not make a vast profit so the real potential must be increasing sales from the show.

Let's look again at the engagement rate. Speaking to one visitor every five minutes seems pretty relaxed. Could we improve that to one every four minutes and how would that affect the numbers?

It would increase the number of visitors engaged with by five per hour or 70 for the two days. This gives us 18 more enthusiasts, 9 more appointments and 3 more sales. I make that an extra £3750 (over 45%) profit.

Can it be done? Absolutely; in my business I expect front-line staff to qualify visitors in less than 90 seconds – that leaves them two-and-a-half minutes to ready themselves for the next ~~vict~~ visitor!

Whether this modest profit will be enough for a greedy FD is questionable. But a profit is a profit and if you want more, you can always ramp up the numbers. A slightly larger stand will enable you to involve more staff and increase the number of engagements without significantly increasing the overall cost.

Winning the Exhibition Game II
Keep on Winning!

Okay, I know I made the figures up and you wouldn't expect me to show a loss, but my figures are reasonable. No umbongo here, honest. And if you make the same kind of calculations for yourself, you will soon be able to see where you have been wildly optimistic (£200,000 sales at the show for instance!) and where you have a fair chance of success. After your first show, experience will enable you to refine your calculations.

The sad thing is, so few exhibitors even try to do the calculations. They have no idea what to expect and are disappointed without ever knowing the real reasons the show did not live up to expectations.

If that last paragraph sounds like you, don't despair. You now have the tools to go back and calculate retrospectively. That's assuming you remembered to collect the data necessary to enable you to calculate. If you didn't remember, you're just like the majority. Either way your next show can only be an improvement.

Winning the Exhibition Game II
Keep on Winning!

REMEMBER

Set realistic targets

Measure your results

Analyse and improve

Chapter 3

Selecting the best show for you

This is where the process of successful exhibiting really begins. There are literally hundreds of shows each year in Britain alone. If you include the rest of the world, make that thousands. Some will obviously be of no interest to you but it is important not to write off any show without considering exactly who will be likely to attend. Many years ago a friend of mine found that housing association exhibitions were very successful for his business. His business? Microfilm! His company took paper records that had to be kept for commercial or statutory reasons and turned them into handy little rolls of film. He reasoned that the organisations visiting these shows, being under strict government restraints, would have lots of records to keep. There was then no more cost effective way of storing information reliably for long periods of time than microfilm. He did a roaring trade (and still does though nowadays the demand is more for digitising than microfilm). You too need to think laterally, as he did, especially if you have a small budget.

Winning the Exhibition Game II
Keep on Winning!

The first question to ask yourself is 'who is my target client?'

Continuing the theme of our software sellers, they are looking for managing directors, financial directors and perhaps IT directors of medium to large enterprises. Having answered the first question we now see that there are a number of supplementary questions that also need answers:

1. What sort of shows do these target people attend?

2. What, if any is the best time of year to approach them?

3. How many established shows meet your criteria?

4. What information can you gather about likely shows?

5. Is geographic location a consideration?

6. Is there anything scheduled that will clash – for your potential visitors or for you?

7. Where should you locate your stand?

8. Would you be better considering conferences or open days rather than trade shows.

1. **What sort of shows do these people attend?**

You can probably make an educated guess, if you know your clientele well enough. Be sure not to overlook the 'lateral' shows that may attract your target though they are not directly about your particular service or product. So, for BizWiz, computer, software and financial shows are obvious, but what about incentives, business travel, hospitality? Indeed what about exclusive exhibitions and seminars that attract top directors by invitation only? Companies that want to promote their products or services with no competition around to distract the prospects often run these privately. If you can identify non-competing organisations already running this type of event, you might be able to persuade them that a contribution to costs would make it worthwhile to have you involved as well.

2. **What, if any, is the best time of year to approach them?**

If your product or service is seasonal, i.e. there are definite peaks and troughs on your sales chart, then perhaps you should concentrate on shows that are scheduled to fit your troughs. Bearing in mind, of course, that the sales cycle may start long before the actual sale is consummated.

3. **How many established shows meet my criteria?**

The emphasis here is on *established.* Don't be tempted to take a chance on a newly conceived exhibition – no matter how positive the organisers are that it will attract just the type of visitor you are seeking. Watch carefully to see whether the right kinds of organisations are there (exhibitors *and* visitors). If it then looks potentially worthwhile, book for the second or third year. To find out whether an established show is likely to work for you, contact the organisers and ask for historic data on who exhibits and, somewhat more important, who attends.

4. **What information can I gather about likely shows?**

Clearly the organisers are going to want you to attend so their information will be, at best, optimistic and, at worst, downright misleading. To get the whole picture, you need to get amongst the 'victims'. Speak to some of the past visitors and exhibitors. Ask them what they thought of the show, how much business they did and whether they will be going again. Note that it is probably best to ask non-competing exhibitors. The competition might want to keep you out and be less than enthusiastic even though they had a whale of a show. (Or they may wax lyrical about a lousy result, if they are really underhand!) Visitors are likely to be pretty trustworthy though. But make sure you get a cross-section of opinion and don't be put off, or enthused, by any one report. By the way, if you did this investigation systematically and sent out a questionnaire to past visitors, with some kind of incentive to respond, you could be adding useful names to your prospect database at the same time as compiling research statistics.

5. **Is geographic location a consideration?**

Probably not for our software seller. He doesn't mind where his clients are situated. But for some of us it is important. Around half the visitors to an average exhibition will be based within a couple of hundred miles of the show. So if your vans only deliver in South Yorkshire, avoid shows in Inverness and London.

6. **Is there anything else scheduled that will clash?**

What company events are coming up that may leave you short of suitable staff for your stand? Is there a sales promotion scheduled that will mean your sales team will be swamped if you add exhibition leads to their workload? Will you need to consider outsourcing the follow up campaign to ease the load on your in house staff? You also need to consider local and national events that may compete with your chosen exhibition and thus reduce the numbers attending.

7. **Where should I locate my stand?**

This is interesting because first thoughts relate to where *in the hall* your stand should be. But wait, maybe you shouldn't even be in the hall. Some organisations have found it works to take a hotel suite near the show and invite prospective clients along for exclusive meetings, privileged previews of new products and so on. It might even pay you to hire a converted bus and put on a road show. But let's assume you want to remain conventional and take a space within the exhibition hall (probably the safest bet anyway).

Typically, the stands around the edges of the hall are small organisations selling products direct. They are hoping to make their profit on sales actually made at the exhibition. The larger stands are the 'big boys'. They are often there just to show off. They spend a misdirected fortune, are inevitably disappointed but umbongo about how great it all was to their competitors who are doing exactly the same thing. They are terrified not to be seen in case everyone thinks they are in trouble and then maybe their share price will plummet and they *will* be in trouble. Do not emulate the big boys. Instead consider the traffic flow (other things being equal, people tend to turn left on entering the hall) and try to get a space that will give you maximum useful visitors passing your display. This may mean you want to be near the 'hot' industries that everyone will want to visit. Or maybe you would like to be close to an entrance, an exit (probably not – they'll be exhausted and eager to get home by the time they near an exit), or a café. Or do you want to be at the top of an escalator, beside the seminar hall or theatre? Only you can know for sure.

Winning the Exhibition Game II
Keep on Winning!

What I can tell you though, is where you definitely do not want to be:

- In a dead end aisle

- Beside a toilet

- Facing away from the traffic

- Behind columns or with columns in the middle of your space.

- At the far end of the hall from the entrance/exit

- In a low ceiling area

REMEMBER

Think laterally to select the best show for you

Be aware of geographic & seasonal considerations

Select a site with passing traffic

Chapter 4

The budget and how to handle it

 The question of budget may be approached from two directions. There is a rule of thumb that says total cost will be close to four times the cost of the space you take. You can decide how much space you need, multiply the cost by approximately four and then try to justify it to the financial director. Or you can allocate (or have allocated for you) a total budget first, divide by four and see how much space that will buy you. *('Not as much as you hoped' is the answer.)*

We said that a rough guide to total cost is to multiply the space cost by four. This holds up remarkably well in practice. Going back to Bizwiz, let's look at how the budget business works for them.

We said that they had taken a 20 square metre stand @ £300 per m^2. That gives us £6000 times 4 = £24,000. Is it really going to cost that much? Easily.

A simple display for our software seller will cost around £5000. Bizwiz is a little more ambitious and decides to include a rolling video display and an electronic text board so we need to add another £2000 to cover them. The cost to transport, set up, dismantle and return to storage will, of course, depend on several factors including size, distance and how long to store between shows. An average cost would be around £1500. Services on the stand (electricity, gas, plumbing, cleaning) could add £500 to the budget – but Bizwiz needs only electricity and cleaning, so let's add £200. Total for display plus services is therefore £8700.

They need six staff in total, working the stand in rotation, Assuming that all the staff are of a similar level of seniority, let's budget £150 per day. The total comes to £2700.

A daily subsistence payment of £25 is not unreasonable (assuming that breakfast and dinner will be at the hotel), adding a further £450. Allow £130 per person per day for the hotel plus travel costs of £50 per person - that comes to £2640.

So far we have managed to add £14490 to the space cost of £6000. That leaves £3510 for Advertising, PR and promotions. Not a difficult sum to spend, especially if you want to be sure of attracting the right kind of visitor to your stand.

The percentage breakdown for BizWiz is therefore:

Space	25%
Display, transport, services	36%
PR, advertising, promotion	15%
Staff	24%

Because of the high number of leads BizWiz is targeting, their breakdown is a little different to the 'norm'. The reason for their strategy is simply that they have a fairly low-cost product on offer so they are looking for a very high throughput of visitors. Hence they have saved on display costs by having a relatively simple design and used the 'spare' budget to increase the number of stand staff. A classical breakdown would be more like this:

Space	20-30%
Display, transport, services	45-55%
PR, advertising, promotion	8-15%
Staff	8-15%

Markedly different, although for Bizwiz it did still come out at four times the space cost. Since I am making up the figures though, I doubt that this has come as a terrific surprise. What it does illustrate is the importance of doing your own calculations, based on your unique mix of needs, rather than relying on statistics (which are always umbongo anyway).

BUDGET CHECKLIST
You will probably not need everything listed here. On the other hand you may have items peculiar to your business to add.

1. Space
2. Display
   - Design and construct
   - Graphics
   - Audio-visual hire
   - Lighting
   - Products
   - Display models
3. Furniture
   - Rubbish bins
   - Coat racks
   - Carpet
   - Equipment rental
   - Flowers
   - Curtains

For a number of reasons I recommend you DO NOT *budget for any of the following though I include them for completeness and because I know many will not take my advice!*

   - Tables
   - Chairs
   - Cabinets

Winning the Exhibition Game II
Keep on Winning!

- Desks
- Laptops

4. Services
    - Set-up/dismantle
    - Shipping/storage
    - Electricity
    - Water
    - Cleaning
    - Photographer
    - Security
    - Insurance
5. PR, advertising, promotion
    - Press releases
    - Mailing
    - Telemarketing
    - Posters
    - Magazines
    - Radio/TV
    - Promotions & giveaways
    - Special events
6. Staff
    - Salaries
    - Hotel
    - Subsistence
    - Travel
    - Clothing & name tags
7. Extra activities
    - Entertainment
    - Training

8. Miscellaneous
- There's always something!
- And then there's always something else!

One final point. BizWiz is spending £24,000 to be seen at a show that is open for a total of 18 hours. That works out over one thousand pounds an hour (£1333.33 for the pedants). YOUR STAFF SHOULD KNOW THIS. Only when they understand just how much you are risking, will they appreciate what faith you have in their ability to deliver the goods. *(Or rather, deliver the leads.)*

REMEMBER

Price times four equals total cost (approximately!)

Allocate sufficient staff – *they* do the business

Budget for *everything*

Let the team know how expensive this venture is

Chapter 5

Planning and preparation

Clearly you cannot simply book a shell stand, turn up on the day with a few posters and leaflets and hope to do well. This is exactly what a majority of small exhibitors seem to do, judging by shows I have attended.

A successful exhibition is the result of rigid planning and tight timetabling. Always remember you have a deadline that cannot be allowed to slip. The exhibition will not wait for you. Unfortunately, your team will probably not be exclusively concerned with exhibitions – they will have other work to do and the show will run alongside this. Your team will also run into unforeseen problems since, unless you have been at the exhibiting game for many years and established a routine, each show will present its own unique difficulties. Come to think of it, even if you *have* been at the game for many years, your team will run into unforeseen problems!

Objectives must be agreed, probably across departmental boundaries. A command structure must be put in place since different department heads may well want to turn the exhibition into a personal project. Progress reports must be circulated so that everyone is aware of the current position and any potential problems. The exhibition team (cross-departmental, almost certainly) must be supported in its efforts.

But first things first. What exactly do you want to do at this exhibition? There are only four possibilities:

	TARGET	
WITH	EXISTING CLIENTS	NEW CLIENTS
EXISTING PRODUCTS or SERVICES	There may be more cost-effective methods!	Good use of exhibition opportunities
NEW PRODUCTS or SERVICES	*Possibly* a good strategy	Excellent use of exhibition opportunities

One of the best ways to introduce an existing
client to a product or service she is not
currently using is to take her to lunch and
make a presentation. How many clients can
you take to lunch for £24,000? Any
questions?

New products or services can sometimes be
introduced to existing clients effectively at an
exhibition, especially if your presentation will
benefit from having a larger audience. But
consider whether you would be better off
inviting a group of clients to a 'client only'
affair. It should cost a lot less than a full-
blown exhibition and may well gain you extra
points because they will feel privileged,
cared for and valued by virtue of the
exclusive nature of the event.

Taking existing products/services to the
show clearly gives you a chance at those
prospects who have been elusive or whose

existence you have not previously been aware of.

Finally, showing new products or services will not only achieve the aims mentioned in the previous paragraph but it may well open your eyes to new markets that you have not yet considered.

Now that you know what you want to do at the exhibition it is time to begin assembling your Exhibition Manual. This invaluable piece of literature is not just going to be a historical record of the show. In time it will become the Company Exhibition Bible, showing future exhibition teams the right way to do things.

The first item in Section One of your Exhibition Manual will be your timetable; all else springs from this. Here is a suggested timetable. Do not follow it slavishly; while it is pretty comprehensive, you will almost certainly have to adapt it to your particular needs.

Months to go	Operations
12	Set budget and calculate required R.O.I. Reserve space.

Winning the Exhibition Game II
Keep on Winning!

	Create and list targets/objectives. Select show team.
11	Decide what products/services to show.
10	Select stand contractor (design/build).
9	Approve design draft.
8	Consider any 'specials' for exhibiting. Review budget. Order specials.
7	Stand design final to organiser for approval.
6	Plan advertising/PR/promotion strategy (with agency if you use one). Don't forget to consider an ad in the exhibition catalogue.
5	Arrange electricity and any other services needed. Order extras like carpeting and photographer.
4	Plan staff rotas. Arrange hotels, travel tickets, insurance. Book cleaners Check PR is on

	time/target. Order printing (graphics, posters etc.) Arrange shipping etc. for display if not already agreed.
3	Begin staff training. Send tickets to clients and hot prospects. Mailshot non-ticket prospects. Stand build should be nearing completion.
2	Issue show manual to stand staff. Finalise staff rotas. Double check *everything* – some things will not be ready so prepare to deal with panic!
1	Final staff briefings. Final press releases.
0	**THE SHOW!**
+1 and on	Post mortem. Debrief staff. Follow up leads. Monitor results against objectives. Book for next year?

In addition to the timetable, **Section One** will contain all the items referred to in months 12 and 11. So budgets, reservation confirmation, objectives list and team members' names will all be included here.

In **Section Two** keep everything relating to the stand; contractors' details, drawings, contract notes. The company you choose to build your display may well undertake the transportation, erection, dismantling and future storage of your display material as part of their service. For most organisations this is the most convenient and trouble-free option, though it is obviously going to be somewhat more expensive than DIY. This section should also contain details of any special equipment or models needed exclusively for exhibitions and of the services ordered - electricity, cleaning and the like.

Section Three will be the PR and advertising section with details of the agency and the campaign, including advertising and promotion schedules.

Section Four relates to the stand staff, outsourced or internal – names, departments and responsibilities together with details of training programmes they will attend. If you are supplying special clothing put the details here. Don't forget the name badges!

Section Five will contain copies of any internal forms used in connection with exhibitions (for example, data collection forms). This is also the miscellaneous section containing anything related to exhibitions that has not found a home elsewhere.

Be sure to send out a monthly progress report to everyone involved with the exhibition. As the exhibition draws closer you may need to increase meeting frequency to fortnightly, or even weekly. Reports need not be long and detailed just so long as they keep everyone up to date and feeling that they are part of the team.

No doubt you will want to modify the Manual in the light of experience. This means a loose-leaf arrangement, preferably a four-ring binder with reinforcers for the holes in the paper – this will be a much-used manual. You may want to increase the number of sections for your own convenience – but what we have so far will give you a head start over the competition, who are not nearly so well organised.

The Exhibition Manual is just what the show team needs – but we must not forget the stand staff. They need something to help

them as well. 'The Stand Staff Manual' fits
the bill nicely.

The most important item in this manual is the
staff schedule, showing who is on duty and
when. For a sample schedule see Chapter 8.

In addition, the manual should include:

- Details of all the team members
  including home (probably) and mobile
  numbers.
- A map of the show area showing the
  venue, hotel(s), restaurants.
- A map of the exhibition hall showing
  the company stand, toilets, fire exits,
  refreshment facilities - and main
  competitors' stands.
- A diagram of your stand layout.
- Details of what is being shown.
- Pricing, including any special
  'exhibition only' deals.
- Scripts
- Objectives.
- Data collection forms.
- Personal training notes.

Ideally, each member of the stand staff
should have a personal copy of the Manual,
though security considerations may mean
that each person only receives the

information he needs in order to do his job
properly.

REMEMBER

Beware of inter-departmental politics

Exhibition Manual

Stand Staff manual

Monthly (at least) progress reports

Chapter 6

Stand design for maximum impact

You want your stand to attract your target audience and no one else. So display a big benefit that only your target audience will be interested in. Some years ago, I wrote a little book for a management services company entitled 'Business Documents – How Long Should I Keep Them?' It is a very boring booklet, but exactly right for the target market which is people like company secretaries who can go to jail if they get this sort of thing wrong. That little book still attracts prospects like picnics attract ants. What can *you* offer that will bring the right people to your stand? That's what goes up front in big letters that no one can miss. Even if it is as boring as 'Business Documents .. etc.' The point is that it is *not* boring to the right people – the ones you want to do business with.

Notice I haven't mentioned your company name. Unless yours is a household name, use it discretely. It may boost your Managing Director's ego to see the name in lights (especially if the company name *is* the MD's name) but it won't do a damned thing for business. No, what needs to be seen is a benefit. Big and bold so that it is the first thing anyone coming even close to your stand will see.

First impressions are crucial to your success. You have only a few seconds to impact a visitor who is not specifically looking for you. Even if they *are* looking for you, most people will give up at a crowded show if you are not easily spotted.

The visitors you want to meet are busy people. They move swiftly through the show searching for what matters to them. I remember a colleague of mine having some leaflets designed and printed by a 'professional' agency. The leaflets were to go on a display rack in a busy retail outlet. Unfortunately the designer had chosen to print on a coloured background that made the copy unreadable unless you held it right up to your face. When I pointed this out to my colleague he told me that the designer had said this would encourage people to pick up the leaflet to see what it was all about. I said to him what I repeat to you, "Umbongo! No, they won't!" If your message is not instantly clear, obvious and relevant, potential visitors will simply pass you by. We are all assailed by so much advertising, so many demands on our finite attention resources, that only the very best, most noticeable and strident can hope to capture our attention for even a moment. Bear this in mind when you consider your display strategy. Discretion is the better part of valour, not vending.

Though you would be well advised to use a professional company to design and build your display, you do need to brief them as to what exactly you require. There are some basic guidelines to consider. First remember that an outsider, such as your contractor, may not yet understand your organisation, what it stands for or what makes it unique in the marketplace. Be sure that *you* do before you try to explain it to them.

Go for subtle colours and very unsubtle graphics with the very best lighting. You aren't trying to win awards from some arty advertising magazine – you're after *clients*. So highlight your benefit message(s).

Make sure that your message will be visible and legible from at least 5 metres away.

Remember that a picture is worth a thousand words (but you *will* need words as well). Talking of pictures, a photograph is more believable than artwork. So use pictures of real clients wherever possible, together with endorsement quotes. Have them pictured using your product, with delighted smiles lighting up their faces. Not only will this give you credibility, it will please those clients mightily and lock them even more firmly into your organisation.

If you are able to demonstrate your product or service, then plan to do so. Demonstrations engage people so long as they are short and entertaining. Make sure the stand design leaves room for some demonstrating. People don't mind crowding together for a few minutes but they do want to be able to see what's going on.

What exactly will you be showing? Some organisations try to include every single service or product. This is a mistake. Visitors are short of time and too much choice leads to confusion, time wasting, irritation and often to lost opportunity. Prospective clients will always ask you about a need they feel you should be able to satisfy. Decide on your primary focus and ruthlessly pare away at the non-essentials. That's what Bizwiz did. They market a whole range of business software but they decided to promote just one package at the show. No doubt though, they will have picked up leads to whom they will be able to sell alternative products.

How best to promote? The answer to that is simple – memorably! Time is short. Winston

Winning the Exhibition Game II
Keep on Winning!

Churchill was fond of saying that a speaker has only 30 seconds to grab his audience by the throat. You have maybe 2½ seconds because that is about how long it will take your prospect to walk past your stand. Tell your stand contractor that you want big, bold graphics with few words. Make sure your stand layout includes a way on, a route through the 'experience' and an exit. There is material for a book solely about stand design (and such books are available); for now we must leave it at that.

Keep it simple and jargon-free. Even the most technically inclined will forget the meaning of a favourite acronym from time to time. No one will admit to it though, they will simply pass on by. So you gaily put up a huge banner saying something like 'Calculate your VAT, ROI and TVD in half the time!' and wonder why no one comes to talk to you. It is because they don't know what you are talking about. And in case you don't know either, VAT is 'value added tax', ROI is 'return on investment' and TVD probably means 'television dinner'.

Say what you mean in language an intelligent seven year old can manage and you won't go far wrong.

Winning the Exhibition Game II
Keep on Winning!

There will be people on your stand - your staff and, hopefully, some visitors. This comes as a complete surprise to some designers. They create a magical masterpiece that looks wonderful when empty. And looks more like a battlefield as soon as a couple of humans enter the frame. Consider how you can ensure that the inevitable arms, legs, heads and torsos do not obscure your benefit messages or block access for others.

Ensure that your design makes the stand easy to keep clean. Avoid surfaces that will show finger-marks, beware of needlessly intricate cut-outs that will attract dust and fluff, don't have small breakable items on show. Think of your stand as your living room and visitors (and staff) as inquisitive four-year-olds. Design appropriately.

Finally, always remember that, no matter how careful you are to plan for a trouble-free stand, you will have problems. This is where the Emergency Kit comes in. Your kit should include at least the items listed overleaf.

Winning the Exhibition Game II
Keep on Winning!

Emergency kit list:

- Sellotape/parcel tape/Velcro/glue
- Cling film/bubblewrap/twist ties
- Scissors
- A Stanley knife
- Pens
- Marker pens
- Paper – letterhead and plain
- Envelopes and mailing labels
- An eraser
- A torch and spare batteries
- Staplers – heavy duty and standard
- A staple remover
- Pliers/hammer/screwdriver
- First aid box and accident report forms
- Nail clippers
- Sewing kit
- Peppermints (after two hours talking the freshest breath smells awful).
- Freshen up wipes
- Paper towels/tissues/spray cleaner

Think of some additions of your own that may be peculiar to your industry or your organisation. You will forget something the first time you exhibit but your kit will expand as you gain more experience.

REMEMBER

Impact

Demonstrations engage people

Emergency kit

Chapter 7

Pre-show PR, advertising, events

Naturally you want your hot prospects to come to the show. You may not be as keen to have your existing clients there, but if you don't invite them, someone else will.

> *Consider inviting existing clients en masse to a special on-stand event. You could make this early in the day when there will be few other visitors (even close the stand to non-clients for a time).*

There are several possible elements to your pre-show publicity campaign:

1. Press releases/editorial
2. Client mailings/emails
3. Prospect mailings/emails
4. Advertising in the Exhibition catalogue
5. Press advertising
6. Tele-marketing
7. Posters
8. Radio/TV advertising

Winning the Exhibition Game II
Keep on Winning!

What you will include depends largely on your budget and the above list is in order of likely cost. In terms of cost-*effectiveness* at getting useful visitors to come to your stand I would grade as follows – 2,3,1,5,4,6,7,8.

You will note that I have rated client and prospect mailings/emailings highly. This assumes that you are confident they will be read!

Clients, of course, should read your piece if you simply put your company name on the envelope. Adding your Show Stand number – 'Visit us on Stand 36 at the Super Software Show' – may help.

Prospects are different beasts altogether. You may find it effective to include incentives, testimonials from existing clients, response vehicles and maybe even a gift offer that they collect when they call at your stand. One highly effective ploy is the 'incomplete gift'. For example; you might send one ink cartridge together with the picture of the very nice fountain pen they will collect when they turn up. Only to be used for very hot prospects, obviously.

In the copy your main benefit becomes the 'headline' and everything in the package reflects that focus. Consistency is paramount. Having decided on your priority for the show, whether it is service or product, you must develop and maintain that theme.

The theme must have high impact, be memorable and highlight your strengths. Strengths that are relevant in the eyes of your prospective clients, of course. A relevant strength can be easily translated into a benefit. For example; 'Our call-out fee is the lowest in the country' = saves you money; 'We guarantee to respond within 30 minutes' = saves you time. Sorry, I don't know your business so you will have to work out your own slogans.

Bear in mind that human beings have one overriding interest – themselves. You must answer the burning question **WIIFM** ('What's in it for me?') over and over again. The way to do this is to *sell the benefits. T*here are only seven things that interest me as a client. Will your product:

1. Save me money?
2. Make me money?
3. Save me time?
4. Save me trouble?
5. Make me feel good?
6. Make me look good?
7. Save me from looking bad?

Winning the Exhibition Game II
Keep on Winning!

Timing your publicity is critical to success. There is no point in running an expensive advertisement twelve months in advance of the show – people will have forgotten it long before the great day arrives. Mailings, on the other hand, can begin relatively early (not twelve months early, though – maybe two or three). The best results will come from a series mailing, two to four mailings at fortnightly intervals. Send out ticket offers early and try to get as many visitors pre-booked as possible. Later mailings, to those who do not respond, can step up the pressure and increase the incentives. That way you do not waste your expensive fountain pens or whatever on people who were going to come anyway. Keep a few pens in reserve though, for those clients who find out about them and feel miffed! Plan for three or four mailings in the run up to the show and be prepared to curtail them in the unlikely event that you find you have enough visitors booked.

All of your pre-show publicity has one simple aim – to get prospects (and clients) to visit your stand. If they are to do so, they must feel that the time spent will be worthwhile. Appeal to their emotions, their needs, their greed. Offer them a reward for coming and, above all, make your message memorable.

REMEMBER

Separate clients from 'casual' visitors

Get your pre-show message across

Visitors are only interested in WIIFM

Chapter 8

Looking after your staff

Exhibition success depends more than anything on the staff manning your stand.

Exhibitions are tense affairs. Working on the stand is stressful and tiring. Your staff is entitled to proper training, proper food and a proper bed every night.

Book good hotels with decent restaurants and give them a subsistence allowance that will enable them to eat well every day. That takes care of the physical side.

The mental side can be a little trickier. Staffing an exhibition stand is unlike any other form of sales effort. Many organisations make the mistake of putting anyone whose department is currently under-worked on the stand. Bad move. They don't want to be there. They are probably temperamentally unsuited to the situation. They are not show-savvy and they *will* let you down.

Alternatively, a company may bring in its crack salespeople. Bad move. They don't want to be there. They want to be out in the field looking after the clients and prospects they already have. They too are temperamentally unsuited to the situation. Sales people are used to meeting prospective clients in a one-to-one setting. They may spend thirty minutes or more on each visit, exchanging pleasantries, discussing topics of general interest and eventually getting down to business. There is no time for that at the show. Stand staff must attract, qualify, make a short presentation, collect information and get a commitment before moving the prospect back out into the traffic in less than five minutes (sometimes less than two minutes!). Sales people are not geared to that way of working and they *will* let you down.

This is not to say that Fiona and/or Brian (see Chapter 1) cannot be perfectly good people to have on your stand. It does mean that they will require special training. (See Chapter 9.) Unfortunately, training is often an afterthought, if any thought at all is given to the subject. Many organisations spend vast sums on space, stand design, hospitality and so on. Then the staff, who are the only ones who can make it work, are left to sort out their roles for themselves. 90% of your success at a show is down to the people manning your stand. No matter how much you spend on your stand and your publicity, all they can ever do is attract visitors. Once on the stand, the visitor is at the mercy of the staff – heaven help you if they are not up to scratch!

Two hours is about the maximum time anyone should be 'on duty' without a break. So BizWiz is going to need six stand staff (assuming they can all handle any role) to ensure adequate cover at all times. Let's call the staff Angela, Brian (!), Charles, Diana, Edward, and Fiona (!). Their schedule might look like this:

Time slot	Staff on duty
09.30 -10.00	All - warm up
10.00 - 11.00	ABCD
11.00 - 12.00	ABEF
12.00 - 13.00	EFCD
13.00 - 14.00	ABCD
14.00 - 15.00	ABEF
15.00 - 16.00	EFCD
16.00 -16.30	All - debrief

The day begins with a brief motivating session to make sure everyone is awake and focussed, ready for the trials of another day. Positive reinforcement and optimism are the keynotes. Congratulate those who have

achieved targets and encourage any who
are struggling.

At the other end of the day it is important to
review what has happened during the
preceding six hours. What worked, what
didn't, what needs to be changed and how to
change it. Address any concerns team
members may have. As with the morning
session, keep it positive. Do not leave
anything unresolved. Everyone needs to be
able to draw a line under the day and look
ahead with confidence to the morrow.

During their break periods, staff should leave
the stand. They should not retire to the back
'office' (if there is one); they should
emphatically not remain on the stand and
they must *never* use a mobile phone
anywhere near the stand. Believe it or not, I
have seen staff step into the aisle and
immediately begin personal calls on their
mobile phones. Worse, I have seen them
making and taking calls *on* the stand.

You may feel that two hours on followed by
one hour off is a little indulgent. Believe me it
is not. Staff members have to be alert,
chatty, friendly and on their feet constantly.
After two hours on an exhibition stand, one
needs a decent break.

Winning the Exhibition Game II
Keep on Winning!

The hour 'off' is not simply for resting though. In addition to looking after their own needs staff should walk the show. They should be checking competitors and looking for good ideas on other stands that can be adapted for your company in the future. If there are seminars available at the show relevant to your organisation, encourage your staff to attend. If you are running one of the seminar sessions, they should all definitely attend – visitors will ask questions about the seminars and expect your people to be able to answer them.

It may seem obvious, but do make sure that your stand team is fully informed. They need to know why the organisation is exhibiting, what is expected of them and how to meet those expectations. The horror stories you hear about staff at exhibitions can all be traced back to poor information and poor training. Presenting, demonstrating and prospect qualifying are not skills that are genetically present in humans; they have to be shown what to do before they can deliver results.

How should your team be dressed? Many exhibitors nowadays shun the traditional suit for stand staff, opting instead for polo shirt with slacks or skirt or similar more casual styles. What you decide will be influenced by your corporate culture. It is certainly worthwhile considering buying special outfits for your staff. It can give a cohesive feel to the stand and make staff easily identifiable. If the clothing is designed so that staff can use it after the show, then that will be a bonus they will appreciate. So perhaps you should avoid plastering the company logo all over the garments! I came across a company once that issued male staff with pin-stripe suits as a reward for successfully meeting sales targets. The stripes consisted of the company name repeated endlessly. Believe it or not, there was strong competition for the privilege of wearing a company suit.

> *BizWiz decides to go for major impact by stressing the 'Wizardry' theme. Each staff member wears a cloak and a pointed hat, both covered with silver stars. They carry wands that double as pointers (with a handy 'wand pocket' in the cloak for storage while demonstrating). Finally, each of them has been taught a different card trick with which to intrigue visitors. These tricks can be used as time-fillers if needed, to allow sufficient visitors to assemble for a demonstration to begin.*
> *You can see that working for BizWiz is not for the faint-hearted!*

Winning the Exhibition Game II
Keep on Winning!

Encourage your team to avoid alcohol for the duration and to get a decent night's rest every night. However, to be honest, they probably won't feel much like partying if the show is well attended and they are working properly. They should also go easy on the coffee and carbonated drinks – it is surprisingly easy to overdose on caffeine at an exhibition!

Once the show is over, of course, you should be throwing a party for them – to show how much you appreciate their efforts.

REMEMBER

Train stand staff properly

Two-hour shifts

Motivate – debrief

Dress/drink codes

Chapter 9

Presentation and selling skills

Exhibitions are show business. Your stand team are there to give a performance. Visitors expect high standards nowadays and a lacklustre presentation will not do the business. Every market is a buyer's market today, and we must all put in extra effort to maintain or improve our share. Make sure your team appreciates this. An exhibition is no place for a shrinking violet. Each and every member of the team must be up front and ready to 'give 'em the old razzamatazz'.

Preparation for the show begins long before the team arrives at the venue. Since this is not a 'normal' sales situation, staff have to be fully briefed in advance. They need to know:

- Why they are there.
- Why the company is there.
- What the company's exhibition objectives are.
- What is to be the main focus of the stand.
- Who the other team members are and how the command structure will work. Team-building sessions

may be required if members come from different departments.
- The layout of the exhibition and the stand.
- Where essential services are located.

A frighteningly large number of visitors (some estimates put it as high as a third) fail to become clients because of unsatisfactory contact with stand staff. Either the staff member did not know enough about the company's products (and there was no expert available), or the visitor was not listened to properly. In a high proportion of instances, visitors report being ignored or say there was no follow up after the exhibition despite contact details being collected.

At one high-profile exhibition in London's docklands, we were hired to visit a number of stands on behalf of clients who wanted an unbiased opinion on the impression their visitors would take away. A colleague and I visited each target stand separately. We were, of course, 'incognito' – mystery shoppers.

Surveys show that the majority of stand visitors will wait no longer than a minute for attention. We spent several minutes touring each of these stands looking friendly, open and interested. Out of over ten stands visited, only two stand staff made any attempt to approach either of us. Both offered a variant on, "Can I help you?" On all the other stands, we had to make the running and *we* were the ones who had to terminate the discussion or we would have been chatting all day (and stopping the staff member meeting more visitors).

On only four stands was there any attempt to qualify us as prospects and less than half used a printed data collection form. In a few cases a business card was asked for – this is not enough information to qualify a prospect! See pages 78 and 80 for an example of the information you need.

An exhibition stand is peculiar in many ways, not least because it is perceived as neutral territory. Neither visitor nor staff member is on home ground, though the staff member has a slight psychological advantage since it is 'her' stand.

In the normal course of events, a salesperson visits the client 90% of the time. He is at the prospect's mercy. He can be kept waiting in reception, interrupted by phone calls or colleagues dropping in to the prospect's office with urgent questions. The time and effort involved in simply getting to the prospect's premises can be enormous. At a trade show, the visitor comes to the stand largely unsolicited. He may have been invited, read a press release or seen an advert but often he has simply been attracted by a stand graphic, a slogan or a staff member's approach. Now you must capitalise on his presence.

You have a limited time in which to get your message across. Not perhaps as limited as I have led you to believe in the preceding chapters but certainly less time than you would like.

We have talked about the 4½ minutes that our visitor has to spare for each stand. In truth he will probably spend less than that on many stands for a number of reasons.

The most common reason for a visitor abandoning a stand that initially looked interesting is that the stand staff has ignored him. Come on, you know it's true! You and I have both walked around displays without getting so much as a flicker of interest from staff, who are too busy with their private conversations, are talking to someone on a mobile phone or are cowering at the back of the stand desperately avoiding eye contact with us.

Winning the Exhibition Game II
Keep on Winning!

After being ignored, the next most common turn-off is the ubiquitous, "Can I help you?" Why do they suppose they have been put on the bloody stand if not to help visitors? But that kind of dumb question will invariably elicit the response, "No thanks, I'm just looking." and a swift departure before the sales pitch begins.

Body language is important. A group of staff members huddled together, deep in conversation, will deter the most interested of visitors. Standing with one's back to the traffic implies that you do not want visitors and hovering on the very front edge of the stand, waiting to pounce, will terrify them. Slouching, hands in pockets, eating or drinking - all of these are calculated to depress visitor numbers. No matter how the staff member feels inside, he or she must appear well groomed, alert, cheerful and friendly. A tall order sometimes, but achievable – for a couple of hours at a stretch certainly.

So what will make the visitor linger? A killer opening followed by a laser sharp mini-presentation. But do beware of moving in too swiftly. If the visitor has stepped on to your stand she will need a couple of seconds to orient herself. Equally, don't leave it too long, so that you seem to be hovering around waiting for the visitor to make the first move. The responsibility for initiating the dialogue is yours. Here are some examples of openings that will draw the visitor in rather than sending him scurrying off:

Opening:

> "Take a card, take any card." (Well, it will work for BizWiz!)

> "Why are you visiting the show today?"

> "What are you hoping to find?"

> "What, specifically, did you come here for today?"

Following on with:

> "Are you in the (*your service/product*) business?"

> "Are you familiar with (*your company*)'s products?"

> "Have you seen our new (*your product*)?"

> "Did you know that (*your service*) can save you £XXXX every year?"

> "Did you know that (*your product*) saved (*their competitor*) £XXXX last year alone?"

"Which of our products are you familiar with?"

Subsidiary questions might include:

"Are you involved in specifying (*your service*)?"

"What problems have you experienced in sourcing *(your product)*?"

"Whose (*your service*) are you currently using?"

"What concerns do you have regarding (*your service*)?"

"How could you see yourself using (*your product*) in your organisation?"

"How important is (*benefit*) in your present situation?"

"What are your two most important requirements in the area of (*your product*)?"

In order to qualify a visitor, you must get him or her to talk more than you do. So pretty well every remark from you should be couched as an open question. Encourage him to expand on any apparently fruitful areas with an encouraging 'hmm' or 'Really?' or by saying something like:

> "That sounds interesting, tell me more."

> "How does that affect ...."

This conversation should be designed to qualify the visitor and perhaps uncover a problem that you can solve.

There is, of course, a comprehensive do/don't list to help in dealing with the visitor:

> Do maintain reasonable eye contact

> Don't do all the talking

> Do smile

> Don't interrupt

> Do ask open questions

> Don't fiddle with clipboard or notepad or jingle your keys/coins

> Do treat even the least likely prospect with respect

> Don't finish their sentences

> Do really listen

> Don't use first names, even if they are printed on the visitor badges

> Do look the part – smart, clean, alert

Winning the Exhibition Game II
Keep on Winning!

Don't end on a 'low' note

Do shake hands

Don't let the stand get untidy

Once you have begun the conversation with your visitor, and you are happy they are a real prospect, you can slip smoothly into your presentation, or seamlessly hand her over to the colleague who does the presentations if that is the set up. Let's look at a sequence that might easily occur for BizWiz.

Visitor approaches stand. He looks at the graphic picturing a smiling worker beside a computer screen. Under the graphic are the words 'Bizwiz CRM packages save you time and money'.

Brian steps forward, "Which are you most short of, time or money?"

Visitor laughs, "Both!"

Brian chuckles, "What are you here for today?"

Visitor parries, "Are you part of Megacorp? I came to take a look at their ClientCare software."

Winning the Exhibition Game II
Keep on Winning!

Brian ignores question, "That's interesting, are you familiar with BizWiz?"

"I don't think so, you obviously compete with MegaCorp though!"

"Not exactly compete – but you'll find this interesting. Let me introduce you to Fiona, she'll explain what we do. Fiona, this is Mr Bloggs, from Darth Vader Enterprises". He could do with a little extra time …and money!"

(Name, job title and company name can normally be gleaned from his visitor badge. If he had not been wearing a badge, Brian would have at least asked his name early in the proceedings. And Brian is wearing his badge – as all staff do at all times lest visitors mistake them for other visitors).

Fiona now takes Mr Bloggs through to the presentation area and runs through her presentation to him and three other visitors who have already been assembled. Four minutes later, Mr Bloggs is waved on his way having agreed to a meeting with one of the BizWiz salespeople to discuss his exact requirements. Or at least he has agreed that a salesperson can contact him the following week. Fiona (or another staff member) has gathered all the pertinent information she needs on the data collection form that will be faxed to the office at closing time today.

No, they don't all go as smoothly as that. But more of them will if you have selected and practised viable openings that will attract rather than repel your visitors. Get out that list of Rudyard Kipling's honest serving men – what, why, when, how, where, who – and use them to construct a selection of opening remarks that will elicit the type of positive response you need. Make sure you have a mini-presentation ready that will give an enticing glimpse of possibilities and have them thirsting for more. They get more, of course, when they agree to an appointment with one of the sales team.

The data collection form is crucial. This will enable your sales team back at the office to talk sensibly to Mr Bloggs from the first moment of contact. There are two ways to use the form; the staff member fills it in or the prospect fills it in. BizWiz are aiming for a high throughflow of visitors so they want the

prospect to complete the form. Here is the
form they use.

Super Software Show – enquiry form

*To save you time, please use the stapler provided to attach your
business card to this form*

Name ……………………………………………………………

Position ……………………………………………………………

Company ……………………………………………………………

Tel ………………………… email ………………………

Please let me have more details of

1.

2.

3.

This enquiry is URGENT/NOT URGENT (please delete as
appropriate)

I prefer to be contacted by O telephone O letter O fax O email

      (please tick all that apply)

Date   Actioned   Initials

Winning the Exhibition Game II
Keep on Winning!

We could do with more information than appears on the enquiry form. If possible, each staff member involved with this visitor should add his comments on the back of the form as soon as possible after the visitor has left the stand and while the details are still fresh.

Wants personal call   O   by ....
                                    (back in office on ....)

Wants literature only   O   re ....

Wants samples   O   of ....

My impressions:

Well qualified? Decision maker? Who currently using? Reason for considering change? Time scale for decision? How keen? Others involved? Budget?

FOLLOW UP URGENTLY O

Visitor's comments:

What he/she had to say – objections, concerns, special requirements etc.

Other information:

Include comments from other staff.

Winning the Exhibition Game II
Keep on Winning!

That is what we want to achieve with genuine prospective clients. But our stand will also be host to the leaflet collectors, junior staff, students and sundry other people who are of no immediate interest. I say immediate interest because that student may one day be a powerful buyer, the leaflet collector and the junior may be promoted to a position of influence. So we do not want to offend them and equally we need to move them on as fast as possible. In the case of group demonstrations this is not too much of a problem. Having identified them for what they are, feed them into the presentation and make the appropriate note on the back of the data collection form after they leave.

One-to-one is a little trickier. Brian and the rest of the stand staff are prepared for the unwanted visitor, including competitors looking for information and those individuals who want to complain about the service or products they have received in the past.

No matter how undesirable a visitor may be, politeness and good humour are essential. An exception (possibly) is when the visitor is from the competition, though even then you must be aware that genuine visitors may be witnessing how you handle the 'spy'.

Winning the Exhibition Game II
Keep on Winning!

Those visitors whose youth or job title indicates that they will not be placing orders can be sent on their way, perhaps with a low-cost giveaway, a handshake and, "Enjoy the rest of the show, Mr Bloggs." Or even, "Mrs Smith, thanks for stopping at our stand. Now don't let me stop you from seeing the rest of the show."

Minimise eye contact and practice turning away in an inoffensive manner - this tends to inhibit further attempts to hold on to your attention. It can also be worth arranging a 'HELP' signal that will have a colleague come over and, apologising profusely, tear you away to attend to some vital problem that has just cropped up.

For the complainer, the solution is straightforward. Listen politely and let them finish. Just being able to make a complaint calms an awful lot of people down. Make a few notes to let them know you are taking this seriously. Ask what they would like you to do. If you can do what they ask, make a commitment. If you cannot do it, make an offer of something you can do and commit to that. If that is not acceptable to them, explain that you are not in a position to help and promise to pass the complaint on to someone who can. Give them your business card, ask for theirs, and again commit to taking action. Then wave them goodbye.

 If the complainer is causing a disturbance, offer to take them for a coffee so as to get them away from the stand. You can explain that it will be easier to discuss the problem in comfort over a coffee. Be positive and friendly, no matter how upset they may be. Always remember that the complaint is not directed at you personally; you are simply the representative of your organisation. In extremis – call security! (That's a joke. If you can't handle the odd irate client, you shouldn't be on the stand.)

REMEMBER

Exhibitions are show business

Standard openings

Get 'em on, get 'em in and get 'em off

Don't ignore, harass or patronise

Collect information

Chapter 10

Literature and giveaways

First suggestion – don't have any literature on your stand. Literature doesn't sell. People sell.

Second suggestion – if you must have literature, order half what you think you will use. Then have your staff search the bins near the show exits every evening. They will retrieve enough of your material to ensure you still have some left over at the end of the show.

I'm perfectly serious about this. Many visitors use literature as a means of escaping from a persistent salesman. "Do you have a leaflet? Thanks, I'll study this back at the office and give you a call. No, don't bother to contact me; I'm going to be tied up for a couple of weeks. Let me call you." Oh, yeah! Pure umbongo. You'll find those leaflets in the bin at the exit; this guy doesn't even need them as evidence that he attended.

Other people use the leaflet as an excuse not to commit to a meeting or a follow up call. If you have literature available, how can you refuse to give it to her? But if you have none, you can simply say, "I don't want to burden you with yet more paper to carry around. I'll have Joe call you tomorrow. He can discuss exactly what you require and then we'll be sure of giving you the right information without a lot of extra material you neither want nor need."

Still more visitors go around collecting literature so that they can show everyone back at the office how industrious they have been. They leave the big, logo-covered show carrier bag in a prominent position for a couple of days then bin it when no one is looking.

Now I should mention the prize draw. This, typically, takes the form of a 'goldfish bowl' on the stand into which visitors are invited to drop their business cards. The 'leads' so generated are then passed to the sales team. Those salespeople with past experience simply bin them while the tyro salesman wastes hours running up the company telephone bill trying to get a flicker of interest. I don't know about you but I take a stack of business cards to every exhibition I visit, and a good proportion of them go into prize draw bowls. I may have not the slightest interest in the product or service; I just want the free toaster. The same is true of 99% of the cards in there. And if you think the remaining 1% makes it worthwhile, forget it. The 1% spoke to your staff anyway and you will find their details on one of your data collection forms. There is only one possible 'justification' for the goldfish bowl; top management demanded that an unreasonable number of leads be generated from the show and this is the only way to achieve the target. If that is your problem, and management is deaf to your cries of 'umbongo', start looking for another job.

Instead of a useless prize draw, you might consider a contest, with a substantial first prize that could only be of value to a genuine prospect.

You can include some questions that qualify each contestant for future sales calls. Make it fairly simple and include a tiebreaker of some kind. You make it simple because you want everyone to win at least a minor prize – that gives your salesperson a better chance of an appointment, when she calls to deliver the prize.

A contest also gives you a good shot at some press exposure. The winner(s) will enjoy seeing their picture in the trade press. Could that be another reason for a visit - to take the picture? You might get them to visit your offices even, for a formal presentation and photo shoot.

Winning the Exhibition Game II
Keep on Winning!

You might do a deal with the exhibition organisers; they print your contest details in the show catalogue. If the first prize is substantial enough, they may even publicise it in their pre-show advertising as a way of generating more visitors to the show. Of course, the eager contestants have to visit your stand to enter the contest. After the judging is over, their entry forms become part of your database.

REMEMBER

No literature (?)

Prize draw – NO

Contest - YES

Chapter 11

After the show

FUF. *Follow Up Fast!*

Time and again I hear the complaint that companies do not follow up on enquiries. This complaint is not, of course, confined to exhibition enquiries, but that is the aspect we will discuss here.

The causes of this failure can be difficult to ascertain. Certainly the problem is endemic in British business.

Sometimes the sales team will claim that the leads are rubbish. This usually means that the enquirer has not been properly qualified – common at exhibitions. The staff is anxious to meet targets for numbers of leads generated, so they will take details from anyone. Perhaps, though, you chose the wrong show and these were the best they could come up with.

Another problem may well be that you did not take into consideration the sales team's existing workload. Maybe they just do not have the time to deal with a flood of new enquiries. This begs the question, if you are so busy what on earth led you to think you needed to exhibit in the first place?

Whatever the reasons, valid or otherwise, every day's delay reduces the chances of your exhibition having been a profitable exercise.

Create an action plan for following up. I suggest that stage one will be to send a letter to every visitor. The letters can begin going out after day one of the show. Thank them for attending and give them an indication of when they can expect your organisation to next make contact. If possible, give the name of the person who will make that contact.

All prospects need to be requalified before setting up a meeting. A lot can change in a couple of days and the hot prospect may have cooled, the order may have been placed in his absence or he may even have been fired on his return. Only once a telephone call has established that this is still a prospect should an appointment be made to visit.

There are many ideas as to how to grade prospects. I tend to favour simplicity. 'A' equals 'hot and ready to buy' so get on that phone *now*. 'B' equals not so hot so follow

91

up once you have exhausted your 'A' category. 'C' equals cool, literature and mail contact only. Depending on how many leads your team is working through, you may even decide to telephone the 'C' prospects. Don't waste too much effort on 'C's though – there are doubtless better prospects already sitting in your sales team's files.

Only you know how long your sales cycle is. It may be days or weeks, months or even years. Whatever your particular circumstance, make sure that all leads are tracked. For example, if you have an eight-week cycle, you should be looking for progress reports after one week, three weeks and six weeks, with a final report and assessment after about ten weeks.

Only by tracking the results will you know whether or not the exhibition has been a success. Only by knowing exactly how successful you have been will you be able to improve next time. Only by knowing exactly how unsuccessful you have been will you know whether or not to abandon the whole exhibition business! Do not rely on 'gut instinct', as many organisations do. That will only tell you how many leads you achieved and how good they appeared to be. Tracking the final result, however long it takes, will give you a sound basis for future planning,

Winning the Exhibition Game II
Keep on Winning!

whether that is planning more, fewer or no further exhibitions.

REMEMBER

FUF – follow up fast

Create an action plan

Track results

Chapter 12

Going international

So you want to spread your wings and take on the world! The ramifications of international exhibiting are really beyond the scope of this book. But with the world shrinking, the Eurozone upon us, and more and more foreign companies invading our shores, going international has to be an option for the near future. So here are a few thoughts to help you get started.

First of all, make sure you have mastered the domestic exhibition before you look further afield. International shows are a whole different ball game. Take advice from a native with the relevant experience whenever possible. If it is not possible to talk with a native, at least find out about local methods from someone familiar with the country (or countries) before you venture abroad.

Etiquette varies from nation to nation. For westerners a handshake is the most common form of greeting. But Asians tend to avoid body contact, preferring to nod or bow.

Winning the Exhibition Game II
Keep on Winning!

The business card is little regarded in the West; a quick glance and into the pocket it goes. Other cultures treat business cards with respect. They may be proffered with both hands (in which case they should be accepted with both hands). Yours will certainly be studied with great interest so perhaps you should consider having them specially printed in the local language, or at least having a translation added on the reverse.

Another embarrassing incident from my tyro years involved translations. My company had expanded into Europe (quite a while before Britain entered the EEC). Proud of our position, we took a double page spread in the leading trade paper with our copy in three languages - English, French and German. Our inflated egos were only pricked when our French and German employees began telephoning the UK office, laughing hysterically and pointing out the shockingly basic errors our translation agency had made. To our European prospects we looked like rank amateurs. Which is exactly what we, and our agency, were. You may wish to have translations made, of business cards, literature etc., and you may feel it sensible also to hire an interpreter for face-to-face meetings or presentations. Whatever you do, don't follow my example. Vet your translation agency carefully and make certain it uses native speakers with a good understanding of your industry.

Of course it is not only words that will catch you out. Be careful that the colours used on your display do not upset or offend. Research the meanings that symbols and numbers may have for your prospective clients. For example, you might well avoid the use of 'unlucky thirteen' in this country – but in many Asian countries it is the number four that is unlucky as it denotes death.

Be aware that decision-making slows down as you move east. In America, for example, decisions are very quickly made and long drawn out negotiations make people impatient. In Britain we are more considered in our dealings – the rest of Europe even more so, though major decisions are still often made at the show. In Asian countries however, the decision making process can seem frustratingly slow and deliberate to the westerner. You will need to take the time to build relationships – perhaps over many visits.

Finally, the good news. Financial assistance is available from the government for organisations wishing to exhibit overseas! See Appendix 3.

REMEMBER

Master domestic shows first

Use local experts, native speakers

Translate – it's only courteous

Check out government support

Appendix 1

General Checklist – add your own ideas!

    a. Budget
-       i. Space
-      ii. Design & build
-     iii. Special equipment
-     iv. Services

    b. Staff
-       i. Assign
-      ii. Train
-     iii. Book hotel & transport
-     iv. Special clothing?
-      v. Subsistence

    c. Publicity
-       i. Advertising
-      ii. PR
-     iii. Direct mail/email
-     iv. Tickets
-      v. Existing clients
-     vi. Give-aways

    d. The show
-       i. Staff rota
-      ii. Incentives
-     iii. Data collection
-     iv. Debrief daily
-      v. Clothing and Badges

Winning the Exhibition Game II
Keep on Winning!

e. After the show
    i. Debrief
    ii. Follow up
    iii. Track results
    iv. Book next show?

Appendix 2

Chapter summaries

1   There are many bad reasons to exhibit
There are three good reasons to exhibit:

> To make new sales
> To make new appointments
> To make new contacts

Senior people (decision makers) go to trade shows
Exhibitions are costly
Exhibitions are (can be) cost-effective

2   Set realistic targets
Measure your results
Analyse and improve

3   Think laterally to select the best show for you
Be aware of geographic & seasonal considerations
Select a site with passing traffic

4   Price times four equals total cost (approximately!)
Allocate sufficient staff – *they* do the business
Budget for *everything*
Let the team know how expensive this venture is

Winning the Exhibition Game II
Keep on Winning!

5   Beware of inter-departmental politics
Exhibition Manual
Stand Staff manual
Monthly (at least) progress reports

6   Impact
Demonstrations engage people
Emergency kit

7   Separate clients from 'casual' visitors
Get your pre-show message across
Visitors are only interested in WIIFM

8   Train stand staff properly
Two-hour shifts
Motivate – debrief
Dress/drink codes

9   Exhibitions are show business
Standard openings
Get 'em on, get 'em in and get 'em off
Don't ignore, harass or patronise
Collect information

10   No literature (?)
Prize draw – NO
Contest – YES

11   FUF – follow up fast
Create an action plan
Track results

12   Master domestic shows first
Use local experts, native speakers
Translate – it's only courteous
Check out government support

Appendix 3

A couple of useful contacts:

Association of Event Organisers

http://www.aeo.org.uk/

Department for Business, Innovation & Skills
Tradeshow Access Programme

020 7215 5000

http://www.ukti.gov.uk/export/howwehelp/tra
defairsexhibitions.html

Finally:

Why not talk to Task Force 2 before your next exhibition? We can help with strategic planning, staff training, specialist stand staff and much more!

www.taskforce2.co.uk

Email: results@taskforce2.co.uk

www.ingramcontent.com/pod-product-compliance
Lightning Source LLC
Chambersburg PA
CBHW051329170526
45166CB00002B/742